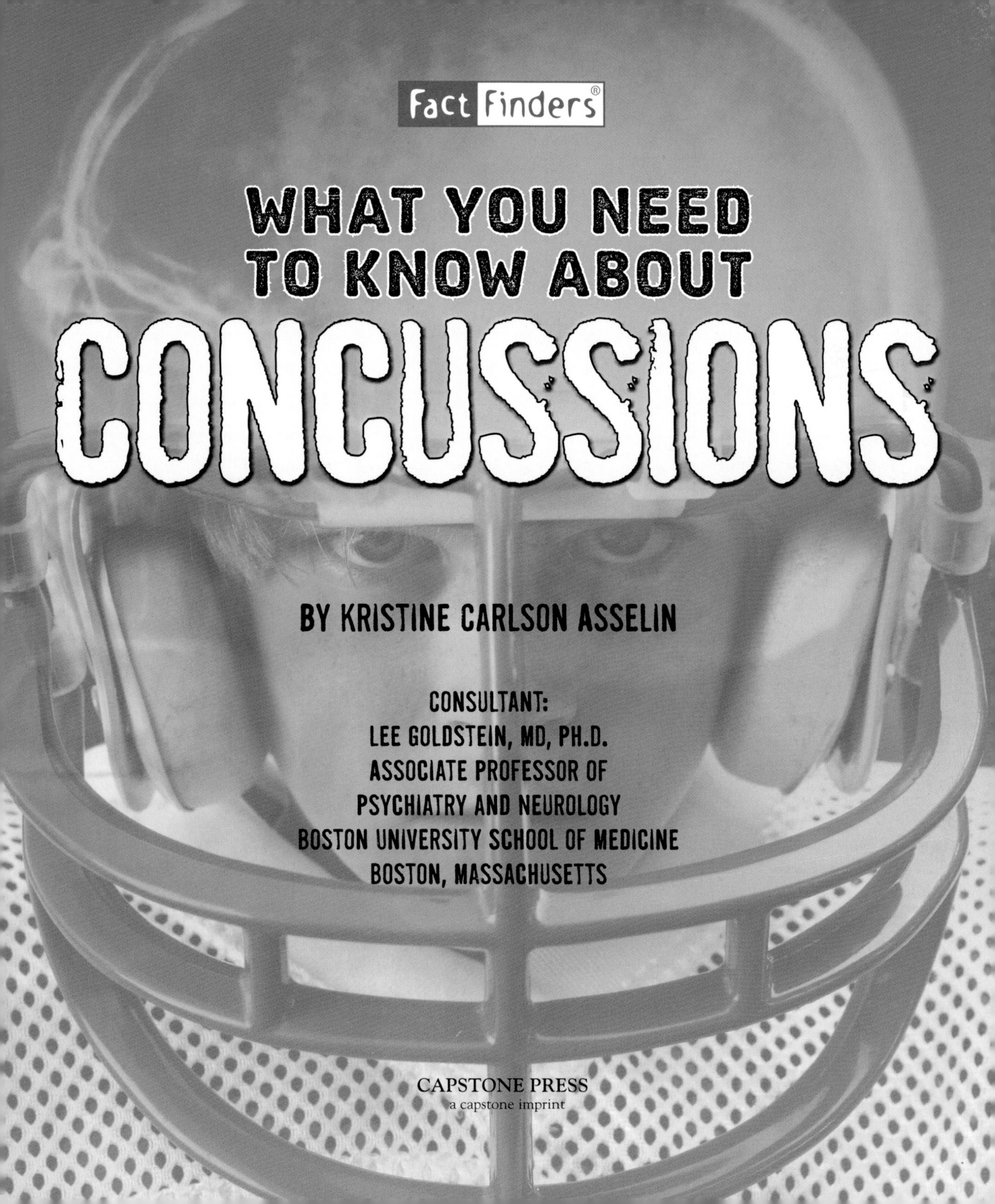

Fact Finders®

WHAT YOU NEED TO KNOW ABOUT CONCUSSIONS

BY KRISTINE CARLSON ASSELIN

CONSULTANT:
LEE GOLDSTEIN, MD, PH.D.
ASSOCIATE PROFESSOR OF
PSYCHIATRY AND NEUROLOGY
BOSTON UNIVERSITY SCHOOL OF MEDICINE
BOSTON, MASSACHUSETTS

CAPSTONE PRESS
a capstone imprint

Fact Finders Books are published by Capstone Press,
1710 Roe Crest Drive, North Mankato, Minnesota 56003
www.capstonepub.com

Library of Congress Cataloging-in-Publication Data
Cataloging-in-Publication data is on file with the Library of Congress.
ISBN 978-1-4914-4834-2 (library binding)
ISBN 978-1-4914-4902-8 (paperback)
ISBN 978-1-4914-4920-2 (eBook PDF)

Developed and Produced by Focus Strategic Communications, Inc.
Adrianna Edwards: project manager
Ron Edwards: editor
Rob Scanlan: designer and compositor
Mary Rose MacLachlan: media researcher
Francine Geraci: copy editor and proofreader
Wendy Scavuzzo: fact checker

Photo Credits
Alamy: Nucleus Medical Art Inc, 7, Sherry Moore, 17, Steve Skjold, 5, Universal Images Group Limited, 26; iStockphoto: ScantyNebula, 10 (left), tacojim, 12; Landov: The Plain Dealer/Lisa Dejong, 20; Newscom: EPA/CJ Gunther, 27, Reuters/Jonathan Ernst, 25; Science Source: Science Picture Co, 13, Spencer Sutton, 16; Shutterstock: Andrei Orlov, 14 (left), Aspen Photo, 4, Bo Valentino, 10 (middle), Brocreative, 29 (top), Eric Fahrner, 6, everything possible (background), back cover and throughout, Jakkrit Orrasri, 9, Laszlo Szirtesi, 11, Levent Konuk, 8, Lisa F. Young, 21, Monkey Business Images, 22, Paolo Bona, 15, PhotoBalance, 29 (bottom), Photographee.eu, 24, Puwadol Jaturawutthicha, cover (top), 1 (top), 3 (back) and throughout, Sergei Butorin, 28, Sinisha Karich, 10 (right), Susan Leggett, 14 (right), 18, Suzanne Tucker, cover (bottom), 1 (bottom), Volt Collection, 23

Printed in China
042105   008831LEOF15

TABLE OF CONTENTS

CHAPTER 1

WHAT IS A CONCUSSION?

It is down to the wire, perhaps the most important play of the game. The quarterback fires the ball downfield toward the receiver. The receiver jumps into the air, straining to reach the pass. Just as he is about to grab the ball, an opposing player slams into him. Both players fall to the ground.

▼ Players scramble during some fast action on the gridiron.

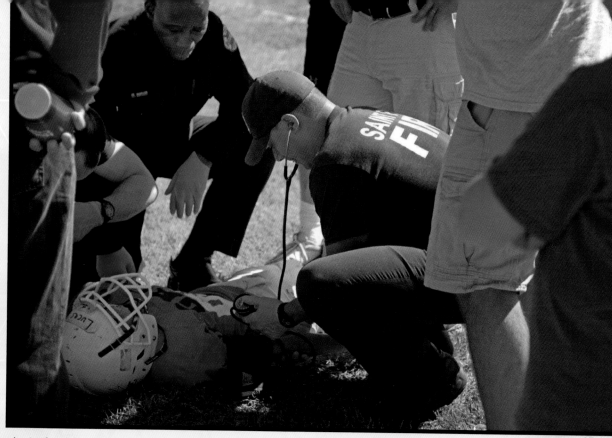

▲ Is this player fit to continue?

Not moving, the player lies flat on the ground. A few minutes later, he sits up. He shakes his head and insists he is fine. He tries to persuade the coach to let him finish the game. But when the player stands up, he becomes dizzy. The coach decides to pull him from the game.

This scene is played out across the country in many sports, for both boys and girls. Even though the player said he was fine, the coach could see concussion **symptoms**. That was why the coach took him out of the game.

symptom—something that suggests a person is sick or has a health problem

BRAIN INJURY

A concussion is the result of a sudden injury to the brain. It is sometimes called a **traumatic brain injury** (TBI). A concussion can happen in many ways. It can be caused by any hard fall. It could be a hit to the head. It could even be a violent shake. Any of these can make the brain stop working the way it should.

▼ A hit to the head or a fall on the ice in hockey can lead to a concussion.

A concussion can be hard to **diagnose**. If a player does not tell an adult how he or she is feeling, the symptoms might not be recognized as a concussion. A second hit to the head, before enough **recovery** time, can cause a more serious injury.

▼ how a concussion happens

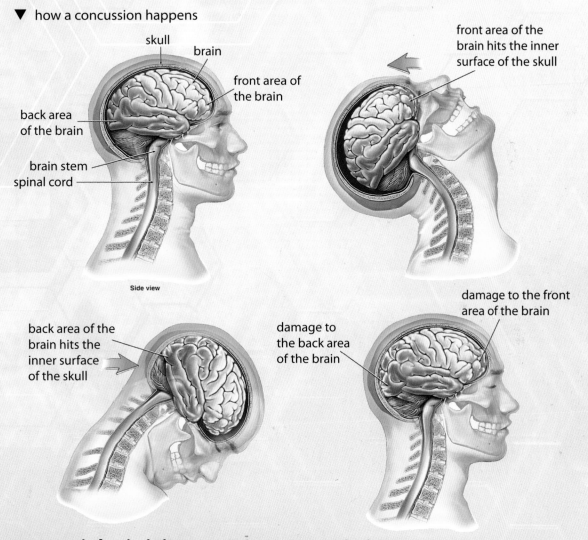

skull

brain

front area of the brain

back area of the brain

brain stem

spinal cord

Side view

front area of the brain hits the inner surface of the skull

back area of the brain hits the inner surface of the skull

damage to the back area of the brain

damage to the front area of the brain

traumatic brain injury—a violent injury to the brain

diagnose—to identify a problem, such as a concussion

recovery—getting better; returning to health

CHAPTER 2

INVISIBLE INJURIES

A concussion is an invisible injury. Your doctor can easily see and treat a broken bone. But you cannot see a concussion with the naked eye. Even modern technology such as **X-rays** or **MRIs** may not show a concussion.

▼ A technician prepares a patient for an MRI.

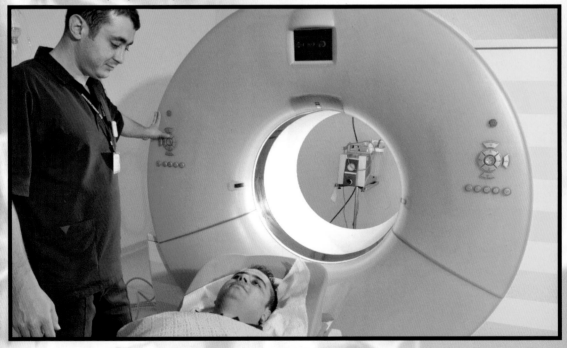

HEALTH FACT

Magnetic resonance imaging (MRI) is a way for doctors to see what is going on inside your body. It uses a giant magnet and radio waves to create a picture. MRIs may "see" problems that might not show up on other tests.

A concussion can be hard to diagnose. Only a doctor or nurse can tell for sure if the brain has been hurt. But coaches and players can watch for signs of concussion. They may notice changes in how a person is feeling, moving, behaving, or thinking. The changes may be **physical** or **mental**.

▼ A player is being checked for symptoms of brain injury.

X-ray—a type of radiation; it takes pictures of the inside of a person's body

MRI—technique that uses magnets to help take a picture of the inside of a person; MRI stands for magnetic resonance imaging

physical—related to the body; something that can be seen or observed

mental—related to the mind or brain

Concussion Signs

After a hit to the head, most people with a concussion may say they see stars, have a headache, or feel dizzy. Sometimes the person loses his or her memory for a few minutes or longer. Over 90 percent of people with concussions were never actually knocked out. Signs of concussion may include:

- headache
- memory loss
- loss of concentration
- dizziness
- loss of balance
- dilated pupils

- nausea
- vomiting
- blurred vision
- swollen bump
- bruising
- mood swings

- depression
- anxiety
- slurred speech
- difficulty speaking
- sleepiness
- difficulty sleeping

▲ dilated pupil

▲ headache

▲ sleepiness

CAUSES OF CONCUSSION

Any hit or jolt to your head could cause a concussion. You do not have to be playing a contact sport. Even hitting a soccer ball with your head could cause a concussion. But not every hit does.

▼ Heading a ball in soccer can sometimes cause a concussion.

Possible Ways to Get a Concussion

Concussions mainly occur during team sports, but there are other ways they can happen too.

- falling off your bike
- getting hit with a soccer ball or football
- being knocked down or tackled
- getting hit with a stick in lacrosse or field hockey
- falling off a surfboard, snowboard, or skateboard
- getting kicked in the head
- running into a tree on skis
- falling off a horse
- skating into the boards (hockey)
- car accident
- playground accident

▼ Falling off a skateboard can result in a concussion.

CONCUSSION STATISTICS

According to the Centers for Disease Control (CDC), there are between 1.6 and 3.8 million concussion injuries each year. Not all of these are sports injuries. But many are. The Sports Concussion Institute (SCI) believes that most concussions happen during games, not practices. Perhaps that is because players tend to go all out in a win-or-lose situation.

According to the SCI, in any sports season, between 5 and 10 percent of all athletes suffer concussions. Kids are especially prone to this injury. Nearly three-quarters of all emergency room visits for sports-related injuries are for young people between the ages of 10 and 19.

▼ When players collide, a concussion can easily result.

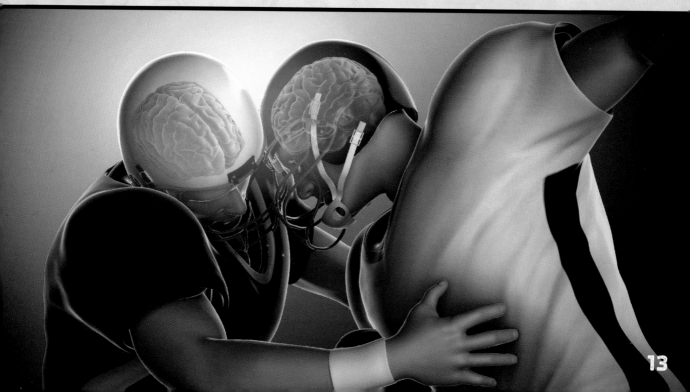

Concussion Rates per Sport

Sport	Concussions per 100,000 Athletes
Football	470
Men's soccer	220
Women's soccer	360
Volleyball	50
Men's baseball	70
Women's baseball	210
Wrestling	180
Baseball	50
Softball	70

▼ baseball

▼ wrestling

MARY KATE'S THREE CONCUSSIONS

Twelve-year-old Mary Kate was playing in an exciting basketball game at school. During the last few minutes she and another girl smashed into each other. Mary Kate got a concussion. Then she fell to the floor and hit her head. That was concussion number two.

Mary Kate's symptoms included headaches, dizziness, and difficulty with her balance. Three weeks later she felt better. Her doctor said she could resume her normal activities.

Seven months later Mary Kate had her third concussion. She got hit in the head by a lacrosse ball. She had the same symptoms she had before. But this time her emotions were affected too. She was moody, difficult, and often angry with her family. However, as Mary Kate got better, all these symptoms disappeared.

CHAPTER 3

DIAGNOSIS

According to the CDC, in the past decade, head injuries for kids have increased by about 60 percent. This is partly because people are more aware of TBIs.

In the past, players and coaches did not think concussions were all that serious. No one had much training about them. So kids were encouraged to "shake it off" and continue to play. We now know that even a single concussion can damage the brain. If you get a second concussion before the first one has healed, you could have permanent damage.

◀ An impact can cause a concussion.

▲ A coach checks a player for symptoms of concussion.

Today there are better guidelines on handling concussions. However, there is still a lot of debate about this issue and what a concussion actually is. Players who have even one concussion symptom are often not allowed to go back into the game.

If a coach or other adult thinks you have a concussion, be sure to follow his or her instructions. If you have a headache or feel dizzy, tell your coach. It is better to be safe than sorry. Having a better understanding of the risks keeps kids safer.

DIAGNOSIS CHALLENGE

Players, coaches, and parents should know the symptoms of concussion. That way, they can make the right decision on the sideline. The wrong decision could mean extra weeks or months of recovery for the player. A player's safety is always more important than winning a game. But how does anyone know if a player should continue playing?

▼ The coach must decide if a player should leave the game.

Suppose the player is you. One of the first things your coach may do is ask you to walk in a straight line or count to 10. Or the coach might ask you questions to see if your brain is working properly. If you seem confused or have any other concussion symptoms, you may be pulled from the game. The coach will ask you to see a doctor.

Concussion Checklist

Unconscious
- Is the player's mouth or throat blocked?
- Is the player breathing normally?
- Is the player's heart beating regularly?

Conscious
- Can the player walk in a straight line?
- Can the player count to 10?
- Can the player answer simple questions?

Actions
- A medical professional assesses the player.
- The player cannot return to the game until a licensed medical professional clears him or her.
- If a concussion is diagnosed, the player is removed from the game immediately.
- The player is to be monitored for 3 or 4 hours (sometimes longer).
- If no concussion is diagnosed, the medical professional may clear the player to return to the game.

HEALTH FACT

To test your memory, a coach or doctor might ask the following questions:
- What color was the jersey of the opposing team?
- What's the color of the sky?
- What's the score?
- Do you remember what happened?

BASELINE TESTING

Doctors now ask athletes to take **baseline tests** before the playing season begins. This is a set of questions and balance tasks. The test records a player's normal reactions to questions and pictures. It also scores some physical reactions.

▼ A research engineer, left, at the Cleveland Clinic works with the C3 app on the iPad2 to do baseline testing for concussions.

HEALTH FACT

A baseline is a starting point. So a baseline test records an athlete's physical and mental abilities at the starting point of a season.

baseline test—a basic standard or level test

If a doctor thinks a player has a concussion, the player takes the same baseline test again. The doctor can compare the results to the earlier ones. Having these tests on record can help the doctor diagnose a concussion. It can also help the doctor judge how bad the concussion is.

▼ A doctor compares test results.

TREATMENT

The main treatment for a concussion is resting the brain. This means no activities such as sports, watching TV, or playing computer games. You should also avoid bright lights and crowded places. All these put strain on the brain, which can slow your recovery. Only a doctor can tell you how much activity to avoid and for how long.

Most concussion patients recover in a week or two. But a severe concussion can mean months, or even years, of recovery. Patients can usually get back to their normal activities as soon as the symptoms are gone.

▼ Doing nothing but resting is the best treatment for a concussion.

Six Steps to Recovery

- complete rest—no physical or mental activity until there are no concussion symptoms for at least 24 hours
- light exercise—slow walking , exercise biking, or light jogging
- moderate exercise—moderate jogging, exercise biking, or weightlifting
- more intense exercise but no contact sports—running, intense exercise biking, regular weightlifting
- practice—full-contact practice
- play—return to competitive sports

▶ Using a treadmill can help recovery from a concussion.

LONG-TERM EFFECTS

Most people who have had a concussion make a full recovery. But without proper care and rest, the brain takes longer to get back to normal.

Long-term effects of concussion can include trouble sleeping. You may have a hard time focusing in school. You may also experience unusual mood swings.

▼ Anxiety attacks are one possible effect of a concussion.

TBIs AND PROFESSIONAL FOOTBALL

Former San Francisco 49ers lineman George Visger thinks he has had thousands of concussions over his football career. He began playing Pop Warner football in 1970 at the age of 11. He stopped playing professional ball shortly after he won a Super Bowl ring in 1981. Because of his injuries, Visger has had many operations to relieve pressure on his brain. Also, his memory is poor. He writes down everything that happens in his life in a small notebook. He cannot remember most things if they are not written down on paper.

▼ George Visger holds a scan of his brain as he speaks about living with brain problems 30 years after his playing career.

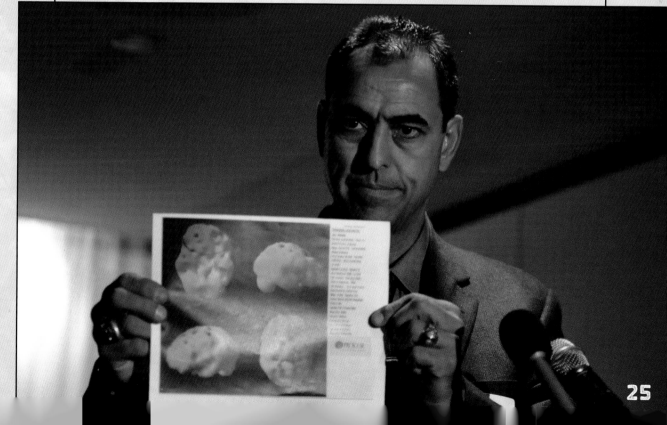

CHAPTER 4

PREVENTION

Doctors now know that concussions are serious. Yet not all these injuries are reported. More than half of all high school athletes may have suffered at least one concussion.

This is why experts want to see a change in kids' sports. Many believe that younger kids should play only flag football. These experts think kids should not play tackle football until high school.

Some experts also want players to wear helmets for all contact sports. However, others think that a helmet does little to protect the brain from a concussion. Protecting the brain should be a priority for any sport that has a high risk of concussion.

◄ Girls wear helmets while playing lacrosse.

TOM BRADY

Tom Brady is a quarterback for the New England Patriots. He is often called one of the best to ever play professional football. But when he was growing up in southern California, he was not allowed to play tackle football. His parents made him wait until he started high school at age 14. They were more concerned about broken bones than concussions. But Tom Brady grew up to be one of the best, even though he did not play tackle football as a kid.

▼ Tom Brady

PROTECTIVE EQUIPMENT

There is a risk of concussion in any sport. You cannot prevent every injury. But it is important to listen to your coach's rules for safety. It is also important to wear the proper safety gear.

Doctors and researchers are still studying the effects of concussions on the brain. But the risk has not affected the number of kids playing sports in the United States—about 45 million. With so many kids playing, concussions cannot be avoided altogether. But with the right information and the proper equipment, sports can be made safer for everyone!

▼ What safety equipment can you spot?

The Helmet

The first helmet was worn during a football game in 1893. A shoemaker made the helmet out of leather. He made it for a player who had been told he might die if he got hit in the head again.

Most games were still played without helmets until about 1915. But even then helmets were made out of leather and fabric. They were not padded well. The modern football helmet weighs about 3 pounds (1.4 kg). It is made from stronger material to better protect the brain. In 1943 the NFL began requiring all players to wear helmets.

▼ old leather football helmet

▼ modern helmet

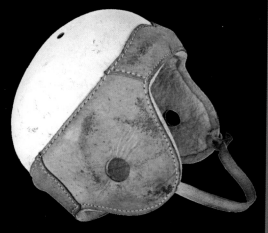

HEALTH FACT

Football players in the early 1900s were called leatherheads because their helmets were made of leather. The first plastic football helmet was worn in 1938.

GLOSSARY

baseline test (BAYSS-line TEST)—a basic standard or level test

diagnose (dy-ig-NOHS)—to identify a problem, such as a concussion

MRI (EM-AR-EYE)—technique that uses magnets to help take a picture of the inside of a person; MRI stands for magnetic resonance imaging

mental (MEN-tuhl)—related to the mind or brain

physical (FIZ-uh-kuhl)—related to the body; something that can be seen or observed

recovery (ri-KUHV-uh-ree)—getting better; returning to health

symptom (SIMP-tuhm)—something that suggests a person is sick or has a health problem

traumatic brain injury (truh-MAT-ik BRAYN IN-juh-ree)—a violent injury to the brain

X-ray (EKS-ray)—a type of radiation; it takes pictures of the inside of a person's body

READ MORE

Goldsmith, Connie. *Traumatic Brain Injury: From Concussion to Coma.* Minneapolis: Twenty-First Century Books, 2014.

Kamberg, Mary-Lane. *Sports Concussions.* New York: Rosen Publishing, 2011.

McClafferty, Carla Killough. *Fourth Down and Inches: Concussions and Football's Make-or-Break Moment.* Minneapolis: Lerner Publishing, 2013.

Watson, Stephanie. *Brain Injuries in Football.* Minneapolis: Abdo Publishing, 2014.

INTERNET SITES

FactHound offers a safe, fun way to find Internet sites related to this book. All of the sites on FactHound have been researched by our staff.

Here's all you do:

Visit *www.facthound.com*

Type in this code: 9781491448342

 Check out projects, games and lots more at
www.capstonekids.com

INDEX